WARFARE

PRAYERS
AGAINST SATAN

WARFARE

PRAYERS AGAINST SATAN

PART I

J. WALLACE

authorHOUSE®

AuthorHouse™
1663 Liberty Drive
Bloomington, IN 47403
www.authorhouse.com
Phone: 1-800-839-8640

Published by AuthorHouse   11/27/2012

ISBN: 978-1-4772-4763-1 (sc)
ISBN: 978-1-4772-4764-8 (e)

Library of Congress Control Number: 2012922430

Introduction

THIS IS A SPECIALLY inspired prayer book that will help believers in Jesus Christ to condemn satan in their daily lives. The constant use of these prayers from the beginning to the end of the book will relieve believers from every satanic interference in their daily lives. The reader will receive a miraculous spiritual and physical breakthrough from God. Lucifer, later known as satan, enjoyed the confidence of God to the absolute extent that the security and guardianship of heaven was entrusted into his hands. In Ezekiel 28:15, it is stated, "You were perfect in your ways from the day you were created, till iniquity was found in you." When unrighteousness was found in him, he developed the attitude of greed and avarice and wanted God to appoint him as regent in God's holy mountain (i.e., the kingdom of God) in place of Jesus. God was bold and frank enough to tell

Lucifer that the position (regent of His holy mountain) was reserved for His Son, Jesus.

At once Lucifer began hating God and His son, Jesus, in heaven. God drove Lucifer from His kingdom and took all his former positions from him. Jesus saw satan falling from Heaven. It is written in Luke 10:18, "And He said to them, 'I saw Satan fall like lightning from heaven.'" Lucifer was, therefore, out of the kingdom of God. In his state of stubbornness, he convinced a third of God's unfaithful angels to follow him to the earth, because in Isaiah 14:14, it is written of satan, "I will ascend above the heights of the clouds I will be like the Most High." He deceived the angels, and he used the same deceit on Adam and Eve, and on you, the reader.

Lucifer, being the perfection of beauty, possessed a personality and charm which he exploited to take advantage of the other sinners of God's creation.

When Lucifer was falling from heaven, he took God as his archenemy and also hated God's highest creation—man. Every believer of God must know that he or she is in a strong battlefield with satan. Satan is an inanity in the life of any child of God, and so he should not be accorded with the importance to write his name with a capital S. God sent his only begotten son, Jesus Christ, to this Earth to condemn satan for His believers. The reader of this book is advised to depart in all his ways from the track of sin and follow or pray in the name of our Lord Jesus Christ as his only Saviour, because when Jesus was born, he was born as Emmanuel (meaning "God with us"). May the almighty

God in the name of our Lord Jesus Christ richly listen to your prayers and condemn satan for you as He did for his son, Jesus. Amen.

Joseph Wallace

CONTENTS

Hints

THESE PRAYERS MAY BE used any time, but the most effective time is from midnight to 3.00 a.m. This is the period during which satan does his wicked acts.

Pray in absolute confidence in your room alone, standing. Lock the doors and realise that you are in complete battle with satan. Believe that you are praying in the name of our Lord Jesus Christ, a name satan cannot stand with.

Have absolute confidence that the Holy Spirit is present with you in the room and will take all your prayers to the Father in heaven.

After the end of the prayers, mention all your requests in areas of your life where you want a spiritual and physical breakthrough (e.g., your finances, marriage life, health, business, etc.), and ask God to give you a supernatural breakthrough, because nothing is impossible with God (see Luke 1:37).

SING SONGS OF PRAISE

*S*TART THE FOLLOWING PRAYERS in absolute confidence by using ten to fifteen minutes to sing songs of praise for the presence of the Holy Spirit with you in your room. Note that you are going to the battlefield with satan to condemn him in the name of Jesus Christ, and so start the following prayers fully charged in your spirit and fearlessly move on with the Word of God, for satan has no power over you any more.

THANK THE FATHER

*L*ORD GOD ALMIGHTY, MY Father in heaven, I stand in Your presence to thank You for Your protection and comfort when satan tried to derail Your divine purpose for me. I stand here in the name of our Lord Jesus Christ, myself, my wife [or husband], my family, and all the believers in You for Your wondrous provisions. Anoint me to pray at this hour and to condemn satan in my life. Amen.

TAKE AWAY SATANIC TRACES IN ME

*I*N THE MIRACULOUS NAME of our Lord Jesus Christ, the conqueror of satan, take away all traces of the behaviour of satan from me and make my body, soul, and spirit a new creature of Yours. I have heard the Word of Your kingdom, and my heart is glued to Your kingdom as it is written in Matthew 13:19, 39: "When anyone hears the word of the Kingdom, and does not understand it, then the wicked one comes and snatches away what was sown in his heart. This is he who received seed by the way side . . . The enemy who sowed them is the devil, the harvest is the end of the age and the reapers are the angels."

Lord Jesus, after reading Your Word, I understood the truth in it in absolute confidence. I understand that satan cannot, under any trickery or lies, take Your Word from my heart. My heart is not like those of Judas Iscariot or Ananias, whose hearts were filled by satan after hearing Your Word.

Lord Jesus, thank You for hearing my prayers. Amen.

Take Away My Personal Devil

IN THE VICTORIOUS NAME of our Lord Jesus Christ of Nazareth, Father in heaven, be vigilant and take away every personal devil in my life. After reading Your Word, my eyes were opened to know that the devil attempted to tempt even You, but he failed. Take away every devil in my life, for it is written in Ephesians 6:11, 12, "Put on the whole armor of God that you may be able to stand firm against the wiles of the devil. For we do not wrestle against flesh and blood, but against principalities, against powers, against the rulers of the darkness of this age, against spiritual hosts of wickedness in the heavenly places."

Lord Jesus, I have put on Your full armour, which is Your Word. I command in Your name that any devil who comes near me be put in the abyss forever until the judgement day of the Lord. Amen.

FEAR NO SATAN

*I*N THE POWERFUL NAME of our Lord Jesus Christ of Nazareth, because even angels feared satan, he has a foolish ignorance within himself that lets him believe he has power over me. In Your name, I condemn satan. It is written in Jude 9, "Yet Michael the archangel, in contending with the devil, when he disputed about the body of Moses, dared not bring against him a reviling accusation but said The Lord rebuke you!!" Lord Jesus, I am proud to say that satan has no power over You and will never have power over You. Likewise, he has no power over me and will never have power over me, my wife [or husband], and my family. Lord, deliver me and my family from every sinful life of satan, and empower us to live above satan in Jesus' name. Amen

---

PRINCE IN CHRIST'S KINGDOM

*L*ORD JESUS CHRIST, THE King of Kings, the King of the universe, the Ruler of all powers, if the devil is the prince of the power of the air, I stand here in Your name and boldly say that I am a *prince of your kingdom*. In the judgement day, the prince of the air will be cast out forever. You will then rule me and Your believers, and we shall boldly walk on a street made with gold. Lord Jesus, I believe You and all Your words therefore answer my prayers. It is written in 2 Corinthians 4:4, "Whose minds the god of this age has blinded, who do not believe, lest the light of the gospel of the glory of Christ, who is the image of God, should shine on them." Lord Jesus, as a believer, I know of Your marvellous powers. In these capacities I condemn satan in my life and in all my undertakings. Amen.

The King of the Realm of Demons

*I*N THE ANOINTED NAME of our Lord Jesus Christ, the King of the righteous, Father in heaven, satan is the king over the realm of demons. I have already declared my position to You, Lord Jesus, that I am Your prince, Your royal, and Your believer. Therefore, drive away any demonic powers in my life. I live in complete unity with other royals in Your kingdom, other believers in Your Word. I am not divided with Your household. It is written in Luke 11:14–18, "And he was casting out a demon and it was mute. So it was when the demon had gone out that the mute spoke; and the multitude marvelled. But some of them said 'He cast out demons by Beelzebub' the ruler of the demons others testing Him, sought from Him a sign from heaven. But He, knowing their thoughts, said to them 'Every Kingdom divided against itself is brought to desolation, and a house divided against a house falls. If Satan also is divided himself, how will his kingdom stand. Because you say I cast out demons by Beelzebub.'"

Lord Jesus, Your kingdom will stand forever and ever and ever to save me and all Your believers from any demonic powers of satan. Amen.

SAVE ME FROM SATAN

*I*N THE POWERFUL NAME of our Lord Jesus Christ of Nazareth, Father in heaven, Your Word has opened my eyes and taken me from darkness to light. This has saved me from the powers of satan unto Your matchless powers. It is written in Acts 26:18, "To Open their eyes, in order to turn them from darkness to light, and from the powers of Satan to God, that they may receive forgiveness of sins and an inheritance among those who are sanctified by faith in me." Lord, I have put all my faith in You and in my faith that satan has no power over me, my wife [or husband], children, family, or business.

In the mighty name of our Lord Jesus Christ, I command satan to leave me alone, because Jesus Christ is my Saviour and Protector. Jesus has assured me that he will not give satan chance to take advantage over me so as to employ his many and subtle devices. As it is written in Job 5:12, "He frustrates the devices of the crafty, so that their hands cannot carry out their plans." Lord Jesus, my body, soul, and spirit are in Your mighty hand. Save me from satan now as You have promised. Amen.

THE DEVIL IS GOD'S APE

*I*N THE POWERFUL NAME of our Lord Jesus Christ of Nazareth, Father in heaven, satan lied on various occasions to deceive me to believe that he is the most powerful in spirit. Lord Jesus, since I followed You, I have realised that satan has no power over You. Because I am Your follower and believer, I command satan to leave me alone from now on. The time when he used to display signs and wonders of falsehood is gone forever in my life. I now live in absolute truth in Your Word. It is written in 2 Thessalonians 2:9–11, "The coming of the lawless one is according to the working of Satan, with all power, signs and lying wonders, and with all unrighteousness deception among those who perish, because they did not receive the love of the truth, that they might be saved. And for this reason God will send them strong delusion, that they should believe the lie, that they all may be condemned who did not believe the truth but had pleasure in unrighteousness." It is also written in Matthew 24:24–25, "For false christs and false prophets will rise and show great signs and wonders to deceive, if possible even the elect. See, I have told you beforehand." Satan imitates God's work and tries by false means to show to the lost that he has the same powers as God.

Lord Jesus, I thank You that You told me in advance the schemes, tricks, and lies of satan. I vow never to follow him, but You. I command the Holy Spirit to assist me to drive away satan from my life forever in Jesus' name. Amen.

LET ME BE TRUTHFUL

*I*N THE LOVING AND truthful name of our Lord Jesus Christ, because You live in truth and love, Your kingdom will stand forever and ever. He who believes in truth and in love fears nothing. As it is written in Matthew 5:37, "But let your statement be, 'Yes, Yes or and Your No, No,' for whatever is more than these is from the evil one." Satan is the evil one and the source of evil in others. He delivers the evil spirit of temptation on those who believe in him. Jesus, You told me in Matthew 6:13, "And do not lead us into temptation, but deliver us from evil one," when you were teaching me how to pray. Lord Jesus, I believe You as the way and the truth. In Your path I will follow forever. Satan, take your lies and falsehood from my life now. Lord Jesus, let my words and actions to You and my fellow men be truthful and loving in Your name. Amen.

TAKE AWAY SIN FROM ME

IN THE RIGHTEOUS NAME of our Lord Jesus Christ, it is written in Psalm 45:7, "You love righteousness and hate wickedness; therefore God, your God has anointed you with the oil of gladness more than your companions." I abhor sin and live in absolute righteousness in the name of Jesus Christ. Lord Jesus, I know from the background of satan that he sinned from the beginning. As it is written in 1 John 3:8, "He who sins is of the devil, for the devil has sinned from the beginning. For this purpose the son of God was manifested, that he might destroy the work of the devil."

Lord Jesus, as I stated earlier in these prayers, I am Your prince. I was born of Your holy blood. You are guiding me with Your sword; therefore, satan cannot plant evil in my heart. This is evidenced in 1 John 3:9: "Whoever has been born of God does not sin, for His seed remains in him; and he cannot sin because he has been born of God."

Lord Jesus, take away sin from me, and do not give satan any chance to plant sin in my heart. My heart should be holy like Yours. Satan, I command you to take away your silly powers of temptation from me in the name of Jesus. Amen.

I Will Never Worship Satan

*I*N THE HOLY NAME of our Lord Jesus Christ, I still stand by my unshaken vow that I will never leave You to worship satan, because satan has no power. As I am Your prince, I condemn satan in the name of Jesus. It is written in Psalm 81:8-10, "Hear, O my people, and I will admonish you! O Israel, if you would listen to me! There shall be no foreign god among you; Nor shall you worship any foreign god. I am the Lord your God, who brought you out of the Land of Egypt. Open your mouth wide, and I will fill it"

Father in heaven, I am listening to all Your directions in my life. I have already promised You that I will never worship satan the liar, the deceiver, or any strange god in my life. You are my only God because You have already promised me, in Isaiah 41:10, 13, "Fear not, for I am with you; Be not dismayed for I am your God. I will strengthen you. Yes, I will help you. I will uphold you with my righteous right hand." Lord Jesus, fill my mouth with heavenly authority and the power of the Holy Spirit to destroy the devil in my life. Amen.

FOLLOWERS OF SATAN

*I*N THE ENLIGHTENED NAME of our Lord Jesus Christ of Nazareth, Father in heaven, as the devil is an evil one, he blinds the minds of his followers from the truth and enlightenment to the extent that the light of Your gospel as the image of God cannot dawn on them. This is a wicked act. It is written in 2 Corinthians 4:4–6, "Whose minds the god of this age has blinded, who do not believe, lest the light of the gospel of the glory of Christ, who is the image of God, should shine on them. For it is the God who commanded light to shine out of darkness who has shone in our hearts to give the light of the knowledge of the glory of God in the face of Jesus Christ."

Lord Jesus, as You are the light, the way, the truth, and the life, I give my body, soul, and spirit to You to let Your glory shine on me. I use the fire of the Holy Spirit to wipe satan away from my life in Jesus' name. Amen.

SATAN IS A COWARD

*I*N THE POWERFUL NAME of our Lord Jesus Christ of Nazareth, I release the Holy Spirit to be around me to fight satan with all the available missiles of God. As I have submitted myself to You and the Holy Spirit, satan is highly resisted in the name of Jesus, and he will flee from me as it is written in James 4:7: "Therefore submit to God. Resist the devil and he will flee from you." Satan, I resist you with the Holy Spirit's fire; flee from me now, you coward! In the name of Jesus, I rebuke the principalities, powers, rulers of the darkness of this world, and all the spiritual wickedness in high places fighting against my bright star from the air, the land, the sea, and under the sea. I command all of you to be thrown into the abyss until the judgement day of the Lord. Amen.

I Am Aware of Satan

*I*N THE PROTECTIVE NAME of our Lord Jesus Christ of Nazareth, Father in heaven, I am aware that satan goes to and fro on earth and walks up and down on it, as it is written in Job 1:7, "And the Lord said to Satan, from where do you come? So Satan answered the Lord and said, 'from going to and fro on the earth and from walking back and forth on it.'" It is also written in 1 Peter 5:8, "Be of sober, be vigilant; because your adversary the devil walks about like a roaring lion, seeking whom he may devour." I use the fire of the Holy Spirit and blood of Jesus to raise an unconquerable standard against that satan or devil who is walking about seeking to devour me. I throw him into the lake that burns with fire and brimstone. It shall come to pass in the mighty name of Jesus. Amen.

SATAN,
AUTHOR OF SICKNESS

*I*N THE WONDER-WORKING NAME of our Lord Jesus Christ of Nazareth, You are Saviour of the universe. God anointed You with the power of the Holy Spirit to heal the sickness of those propelled by the devil. Satan cannot heal, but as a destroyer he can inflict sickness on people. Lord Jesus, I believe You. I use Your blood and the Holy Spirit's fire to wipe away any satanic disease any messenger of satan has been instructed to inflict on me, my wife [or husband], and my family. It is written in Acts 10:38, "How God anointed Jesus of Nazareth with the Holy Spirit and with power, who went about doing good and healing all who were oppressed by the devil, for God was with Him." Lord Jesus Christ, take away every disease or sickness from my body now. Amen.

SATAN,
AUTHOR OF DEATH

*I*N THE GLORIOUS NAME of our Lord Jesus Christ of Nazareth, Father in heaven, You condemned satan's power of death over me for me when You rose from Your death after the third day. Every cemetery, every funeral, and every separation of death owes its existence to the devil because devil is the evil one. Through this, You have rendered satan powerless for me as it is written in Hebrews 2:14: "Inasmuch then as the children have partaken of flesh and blood, He Himself likewise shared in the same, that though death He might destroy him who had the power of death, that is the devil."

I use the Holy Spirit's fire to wipe away all demonic powers of death against my life. I rebuke all the demons that have taken over the contract from satan to terminate my life on this earth. May these demons be kept in the abyss until the judgement day of the Lord. Amen.

SATAN,
LORD OF TEMPTATIONS

*I*N THE VICTORIOUS NAME of our Lord Jesus Christ, Father in heaven, as satan is the evil one in the life of all men, he tempts men to do wrong and evil things against You. Lord Jesus, lead me not into temptation, but deliver me from evil. Satan sought to tempt You, and of that the following is written in Matthew 4:3, 8–9: "Now when the tempter came to Him, he said, 'If you are the son of God, command that these stones become bread' . . . Again, the devil took Him up on an exceedingly High mountain, and showed Him all the kingdoms of the world and their glory. And he said to Him, 'All these things I will give you if you will fall down and worship me.'" In all these temptations, satan never succeeded against You. Lord Jesus, clothe me with Your flag of victory to throw away all forms of temptation satan will lead me into as You threw satan away when You said to him in Matthew 4:4, 7, 10, "But He answered and said, 'It is written, "Man shall not live by bread alone, but by every word that proceeds from the mouth of God"' . . . Jesus said to him, 'it is written again, "You shall not tempt the Lord your God"' . . . Then Jesus said to him, 'Away with you, Satan! For it is written, "You shall worship the Lord your God and Him only you shall serve."'" Lord Jesus, You are righteous; that is why all satanic temptations on You failed. Lord, make me righteous so as not to fall into the temptations of satan. Amen.

THE SOWN SEED

*I*N THE POWERFUL NAME of our Lord Jesus Christ of Nazareth, when Your seed is sown in my heart, satan has no chance to uproot it from my heart. Lord, this is my promise to You. I am a believer of Your Word. It is written in Mark 4:14–16, "The Sower sows the word. And these are the ones by the wayside where the word is sown. When they hear, Satan comes immediately and takes away the word that was sown in their hearts. These likewise are the ones sown on stony ground who, when they hear the word, immediately receive it with gladness." Lord Jesus, You told me in Mark 4:26–27, "And He said, 'The kingdom of God is as if a man should scatter seed on the ground, and should sleep by night and rise by day, and seed should sprout and grow, he himself does not know how.'" Lord, guide me over the seed sown in my heart. Lord Jesus, Your work is wonderful in my life because I have taken Your Word, which is my sword against satan. I make this everlasting pronouncement against satan. Satan, move away from me because I have a dangerous weapon against you in the mighty name of Jesus. Amen.

Away from Satanic Churches

*I*N THE TRUTHFUL NAME of our Lord Jesus Christ of Nazareth, Father in heaven, satan, as king of liars, will mislead the unrighteous and the blind, step by step, into doom with falsehood. In so doing, he gets his churches and his ministers to mislead the unrighteous and the blind as it is written in 2 Corinthians 11:14–15: "And no wonder, for Satan himself transforms himself into an angel of lights. Therefore it is no great thing if his ministers also transform themselves into ministers of righteousness whose end will be according to their works." Lord Jesus, protect me from all these tricks of satan and his ministers so as not to fall into his traps or belong to any of his churches. Lord Jesus, make me a spiritual superheavyweight against satan and his falsehood. I use the Holy Spirit's fire to wipe satan and his messengers and servants away from my life forever and ever in the mighty name of Jesus. Amen. Lord Jesus, I am aware and mindful of the schemes of satan. I use the blood of Jesus to electrify myself against the schemes and the evil teachings of satan. I use the Holy Spirit's missiles and bombs to destroy satanic gatherings and churches in Jesus' name. Amen.

PROTECTION OF MY FAMILY

*I*N THE PROTECTIVE NAME of our Lord Jesus Christ of Nazareth, Heavenly Father, I invite the Holy Spirit's fire to burn alive all messengers of satan working to derail and frustrate the divine destiny of my family. God Almighty, You are the God of my family. As it is written in Jeremiah 31:1, "'At the same time,' says the Lord, 'I will be the God of all the families of Israel; and they shall be my people.'" Lord, we are Your people; therefore, save us with Your protective powers from satan. Guide every member of my family from greed, avarice, hatred, untimely death, poverty, and misunderstanding, and protect our destiny, which You have planned for us as it is written in Jeremiah 29:11: "For I know the thought that I think toward you, says the Lord, thoughts of peace and not of evil, to give you a future and a hope."

Lord, I know that satan inflicts calamities on people, but so long as my family is in Your powerful hands, no member of my family fears any calamity from satan. We await Your destined plans for us that will give the family a future and hope. I use the power of Jesus to condemn satan and any demonic powers in the life of my family. Lord, bless my family as You blessed the family of Abram in Genesis 12:3: "I will bless those who bless you, and I will curse him who curses you. And in you all the families of the earth shall be blessed."

Holy Spirit, on my family gate put a sign reading "No Entry, No Stopping, No Parking, and No Waiting" for satan and any demonic powers. Make the place a dangerous zone for satan and his accomplices. There is no compromise with satan on anything in my life, in Jesus' name. Amen.

AGAINST UNTIMELY DEATH

*I*N THE PROTECTIVE NAME of our Lord Jesus Christ of Nazareth, Our Father in heaven, "The pangs of death surrounded me, and the floods of ungodliness made me afraid" (Psalm 18:4), but You have assured me, Lord, that death has no power over me because You conquered death for me and any believer when You rose from Your death. It is written in Psalm 118:17 that a believer must have the faith that he shall not die but live to declare the works of the Lord. By faith in the Lord I will not die any untimely death, in the mighty name of Jesus. Amen.

CURSE TO THE CURSER

*I*N THE MIGHTY NAME of our Lord Jesus Christ of Nazareth, our Heavenly Father, You covenanted with my great-great-grandfather (Abram) that you will curse those who will curse him (see Genesis 12:3). As Abram is my great-great-grandfather, I stand on Your Word by faith and say that You will curse anybody who curses me. Any evil power pronouncing any curse on me will receive the curse back on him or her in Jesus' name. It is written in Galatians 3:13–14, "Christ has redeemed us from the curse of the law having become a curse for us (for it is written "Cursed is everyone who hangs on a tree), that the blessing of Abraham might come upon the gentiles in Christ Jesus that we might receive the promise of the Spirit through faith." Lord God Almighty, by faith any person from my father's family, my mother's family, my in-laws' family, or any other person who has pronounced a curse against me, I cancel it in the mighty name of Jesus (see Isaiah 54:17) and send the curse pronounced on me back to him or her one thousand times in Jesus' mighty name. Amen.

PROTECTION OF MY BUSINESS AND FINANCE

*I*N THE PROTECTIVE NAME of our Lord Jesus Christ of Nazareth, Lord Jesus, You have the divine protective power to give wealth, as is written in Deuteronomy 8:18, "And you shall remember the Lord your God, for it is He who gives you power to get wealth that may establish His covenant which He swore to your fathers, as it is this day." Lord Jesus, satan has no power to make wealth. He can only destroy, as is written in Job 1:9–11: "So Satan answered the Lord and said, 'Does Job fear God for nothing? Have you not made a hedge around him, around his household, and around all that he has on every side? You have blessed the work of his hands and his possessions have increased in the land. But now stretch out your hand and touch all that he has and he will surely curse you to your face.'"

Lord Jesus, I know from Your Word that You have the power to give wealth, blessings, riches, and prosperity. I also know that You have given me wealth and riches, prosperity, blessings, and long life because Your righteousness will endure forever in my house and in my business. The beauty of my confidence in You is that You have given me the keys to the kingdom of heaven as it is written in Matthew 16:19: "And I will give you the keys of the kingdom of heaven; and whatever you bind on earth will be bound in heaven; and whatever you loose on earth be loosed in heaven."

Lord Jesus, thank You for giving me the keys to Your Father's wealth. Satan is envious about me. I bind all powers, wickedness, rulers of the darkness of this world, and all principalities on earth, and I loose myself from satan in Jesus' name. Amen.

THE CURSE ON SATAN

*I*N THE OMNIPOTENT NAME of our Lord Jesus Christ of Nazareth, Father in heaven, I use Your immutable power to curse satan to remain in the bottomless pit until the judgement day of the Lord. It is written in Genesis 3:14, "So the Lord God said to the serpent, 'Because you have done this, you are cursed more than all the cattle. And more than every beast in the field; on your belly you shall go, and dust shall you eat all the days of your life.'"

Lord Jesus, I curse satan with Your unquenchable power because of his evil and unrighteousness against Your creation. He cannot create but can destroy. Lord Almighty, any attempt by satan to destroy my destiny shall be cursed on him a thousand times as it is written in Revelation 20:2: "He laid hold of the dragon, that serpent of old, who is the Devil and Satan, and bound him for a thousand years."

Lord Jesus, I use Your matchless powers to bind satan for one thousand years of my life and for my descendants. Prepare the eternal fire for the devil and his messengers as it is written in Matthew 25:41: "Then he will also say to those on the left hand, 'Depart from me, you cursed, into the everlasting fire prepared for the devil and his angels.'" Lord Jesus, thank You for condemning satan for me forever in my life. Amen.

THE EXHIBITIONS OF
THE LORD'S POWER

*I*N THE POWERFUL NAME of the Lord Jesus Christ of Nazareth, thank You for condemning satan openly for everyone to know that truly You are the Son of the Most High. Because of Your holiness, You have the powers of Your Father. You have brought satan to nought through Your death on the cross, as it is written in Colossians. 2:15: "Having disarmed principalities and powers, He made a public spectacle of them, triumphing over them in it."

Lord Jesus, now that You have displayed Your powers openly, inflict Your merciless judgement on satan for me and cast him out of my life in Your name. Hallelujah in the highest because Lord Jesus has cast out satan in my life as assured in Luke 10:18–19: "And he said to them, 'I saw Satan fall from heaven like lightning. Behold I give you authority to trample on serpents and scorpions, and over all the power of the enemy, and nothing shall by any means hurt you.'" Lord Almighty, thank You for giving me the authority to tread on satan. I will uphold this authority throughout the whole of my life in Jesus' name. Amen. I boldly say, Lord, satan is already a conquered enemy in Your name. Amen.

SATAN IN CHAINS

*I*N THE VICTORIOUS NAME of our Lord Jesus Christ of Nazareth, victory is now registered in my life in Your name. As You have given me the power to tread upon serpents and scorpions and over all the power of the enemy, bruise satan under my feet and bind him with great chains and cast him into the abyss for one thousand years for me and all Your believers as it is written in Revelation 20:1–3: "Then I saw an angel coming down from heaven, having the key of the bottomless pit and great chain in his hand. He laid hold of the dragon that serpent of old, who is the Devil and Satan and bound him for thousand years and he cast him into the bottomless pit, and shut him up, and set a seal on him, so that he should deceive the nations no more till the thousand years were finished; But after these things he must be released for a little while."

Lord, I rebuke all manner of wickedness, evil, and demonic powers in my life in Jesus' name. Satan is in chains in my life for one thousand years. Victory is in my hand in all the undertakings in my life in Jesus' name. Amen.

THE END OF SATAN

*I*T IS WRITTEN IN 1 Chronicles 29:11, "Yours, O Lord, is the greatness, the power and the glory. The victory and the majesty. For all that is in heaven and in earth is yours: Yours is the kingdom, O Lord, and you are exalted as head over all."

Lord, You are the Lord of all and over all. Satan is doomed forever and will be languishing in the lake of fire and brimstone and will be tormented day and night forever and ever in my life as it is written in Revelation 20:10: "And the devil who deceived them was thrown into the lake of fire and brimstone, where the beast and false prophets are; and they will be tormented day and night forever and ever." Lord, You are the greatest over satan. You are the Alpha and the Omega. Lord Jesus will reign forever and ever as it is written in Revelation 11:15: "And the Seventh angel sounded; and there arose loud voices in heaven saying, 'The Kingdom of the world has become the kingdom of our Lord and His Christ and He will reign forever and ever.'"

I invite Lord God Almighty, our Lord Jesus Christ, the Holy Spirit, and the twenty-four elders in heaven to join me in these prayers and boldly say that the days of satan are ended forever and ever in my life and, for that matter, in the life of all believers of Jesus Christ. Amen. I now yield to the Lord Jesus Christ for my salvation. Amen.

SPECIAL PRAYER REQUESTS

MENTION ALL YOUR SPECIAL requests you want God Almighty to do for you. Use these prayers at least three times a week, and wait for God's plans for you as he has promised in Jeremiah 29:11–13. When you receive a supernatural breakthrough, testify this openly for God to know that you have appreciated his response to your prayers. Remember that God will answer your prayers at his own best time for you as it is written in Ecclesiastes 3:1.

THANK GOD

*L*ORD GOD ALMIGHTY, I thank You for Your patience in listening to my prayers today. Give me Your supernatural breakthrough in my life. Amen.

. . . . Grace

$\mathcal{T}$HE GRACE OF OUR Lord Jesus Christ, the love of God, and the fellowship of the Holy Spirit be with me now and for evermore. Amen.

Surely good angels of God and their mercies are following me all the days of my life as I dwell in the house of the Lord forever and ever and ever in Jesus' name. Amen.